Mother Ship

poems by

Paul Jaskunas

Finishing Line Press
Georgetown, Kentucky

FINISHING LINE PRESS

www.finishinglinepress.com

Mother Ship

This book is dedicated to my parents.

ACKNOWLEDGMENTS

I extend my gratitude to the editors of the journals that have published the following,
often in in slightly different form:

"Mother Ship", "Lenin Square" and "The Wrong House"—*The Vilnius Review*
"Caught in the Lethe"—*Tab: The Journal of Poetry & Poetics*
"Our Questions"—*Ekphrasis Magazine*
"If/Then"—*Five South*
"Come to the Table"—*Pensive*
"Moose"—*The Comstock Review*
"Chanterelles"—*The Hyacinth Review*
"Vilnius to Warsaw, 2001"—*Fare Forward*
"Airspace in Wartime"—*Panorama: The Journal of Travel, Place & Nature*
"A Village No More"—*Panel*
"The Remnant"—*The Windhover*
"Criminals" and "Clouds Like Muscles"—*The Pierian*
"Like a Thief in the Night"—*Amethyst Review*

I wish to thank John Barry, Mikita Brottman, Amy Eisner, Jane Lewty, Saul Myers,
and especially Jennifer Wallace for reading and commenting on my poems over the
past few years. Thank you, also, to Anne Haven McDonnell, whose Orion workshop
helped inspire several of these poems, and to Trudy Hale for her hospitality at The
Porches.

The Dante line cited in "Come to the Table" is borrowed from D.M. Black's
translation of *Purgatorio* (NYRB Classics, 2021).

Publisher: Leah Huete de Maines
Editor: Christen Kincaid
Cover Art: Katherine Bradford, *Mother Ship*, 2006, oil on canvas.
Author Photo: Andrew Copeland
Cover Design: Elizabeth Maines McCleavy

Order online: www.finishinglinepress.com
also available on amazon.com

Author inquiries and mail orders:
Finishing Line Press
PO Box 1626
Georgetown, Kentucky 40324
USA

Contents

Mother Ship

—after Katherine Bradford's painting (on cover)

Ten swimmers tread the blue sea,
watching their mother
ship float off.

Each one, a Moses,
holds a commandment on her tongue
inside her closed mouth.

Nothing here can be said or known
but the mother ship soon to,
sure to, never to

reach the edge of their world.
Her hull, heavy with love, hovers on the waves,
shedding light as she plows the field of blue truth.

She leaves behind her children
to obey one lasting
commandment:

Stay afloat.

Caught in the Lethe

Bramble crowds the banks of the Lethe.

Mulberry boughs and long-necked nettles
and azaleas skirt the river's skin, snagging
debris on the move downstream.

Here comes a lonely bedroom slipper
walking the current with uneven steps.

A telephone cord slithers
along the water's edge.

Next floats an armada of plastic bottles,
a tangle of cassette tape and twig,
and water-logged hairnets dragging vines,
and a hollow doll's head with blinking eyes.

Caught in the arms of a fallen sycamore,
our mementoes commune and bob
in Lethe's slow eddies,

where they belong,
where they have always been headed.

The secret purpose of things
made by unknowing hands—

to ride the watersheds of the earth,
into oblivion's current, where swill
and soot will pull them down
to the riverbed rocks—

to be remembered
by Lethe, if not by us.

Once in a Canyon

Once, an elk loped long miles through a shadowed
canyon, where last hours of light warmed
the red cliffs bearing the marks made
by a people who spoke a tongue
no one living knows—

who spoke to gods
you might well have passed
and failed to recognize on the streets
of your city, on your way to a meeting, where you pushed
about papers, made plenty of sense, and gazed
out a window at the curve
of a cloud...

        Meanwhile, the elk.

 Meanwhile, a boy
        climbs to the top of that cliff,
                looks out and says
        Wow
and
        Do animals also look out and say
                       wow?

Far below him, the elk's loping traces
a sign on the dark canyon floor,
a mark only lost gods
know how to read.

Our Questions
—After Sally Mann's Picnic

The sky has always waited over us,
a question changing its colors.
Gray to white to blue
to ever-baffled night
asking, asking—

with the out-flung arms of clouds,
and confused constellations of stars,
and tears that gather in puddles
at our feet—

of what is our hour worthy?

We have never seen the sky like this,
we have never seen it stifled by smoke.
Crop soot gives up its black answers.

The sky has gone mute.
The sun turns away from us children
who have come to the field
with our hopes
and soft picnic blankets
to celebrate the hour.

I hold my baby in my arms.
It has become a doll.
Its plastic eyes gape at the air.

We watch as the fire reduces
our questions to ash.

If / Then

If the snow leopard crawls into history and never comes out,

and no rodent fears the soft tread of his paw,

and mention of snow leopards falls out of all books,

and all books fall off their shelves,

and the readers of books go the way of dunes on the shore,

and whales that once breached no longer breach,

and tides reach out to swallow your home,

and the bells of the churches go unrung in their belfries,

and the words for *bell* and *whale* and *snow leopard* and *home* sink into the earth like rain—

Passersby in the City

We passersby, each
with a face inscribed
in the minor key of the age,

enjoin our festive noise
to the movement of the hour.
It is scoreless and mighty.

Tympani thrum up all the dank alleys.
A cello tumbles
down emergency stairs.

Let's not call it a warning.
Nor omen, nor song.
We can't even find the orchestra.

Nothing but scattered discordance.
Manic flutes tuned to traffic jams
and hurricanes.

Trombones sobbing
at the cinder-flecked sky.
Beneath all, a phantom hum—

the wordless prayers of beings unborn,
already sick with the air we breathe.
No one hears them.

Everywhere in this city
the concussed, concussing hour vibrates
through concrete walls. We passersby

yet smile and nod and shake
hands with a feral future
just now beginning to snarl.

We would be children and blameless.
Our bland faces blink at the sun
like every starving leopard's does.

Even now beasts of prey
slink andante,
through our streets.

They scavenge the fractured melodies
of our slow catastrophe,
and come night,

under the unhearing moon,
howl their own
crazed counterpoint.

Lethe

Even on the banks of the River Lethe,
our swill foams yellow and green.

The oily sheen of a century's forgetting
scares off the storks and ducks.

In the tall reeds, deep in the muck,
frogs remember all in their poisoned loins.

No more an elixir,
no more the sip of oblivion.

Lethe carries in her current
an unforgettable story.

A machine in every garden.
A coal train screeching through the valley of time.

Adam devouring every last apple.
A fetus astir in a polluted womb.

On the banks of the River Lethe,
the newly dead drink in vain.

Water dripping from their chins,
they wander into eternal death,

awake forever to their sins,
thirsty yet for innocence.

Come to the Table

I've been given too much—haven't I?
I've taken too much—of course.

How many cups of coffee?
How many gallons of gasoline?
How many cows and chickens and trees?

Flights to the other side of the earth.
Feasts on every occasion.
Warmth in every room.

Dante says, "You, although free, are subject."

I pretend not to know it.
I sleep in the habits of comfort.
It is past time to wake up.

Past time to abstain,
to be a bit hungry,
a bit cold and grateful
for the modest gifts of the hour.

You are not a god.
You are not special. One of billions
here now, of more billions behind you
and more ahead, all traipsing
under the same delicate atmosphere.

Submit graciously to the limits of the earth.
Come to the table of brotherhood.
Look into the eyes of your ancestors,
and the eyes of your countless descendants.

Celebrate with them,
break bread with them,
drink the cold water
from underground rivers of time.

You need less than you think.
A portion of soup,
a portion of laughter,
a song to sing.

Come to the table.
Here there is joy to be had, and nourishment
to remind you of your earliest days,
when your mother provided all in abundance.

Yes, come to the table now.
There is no time to waste.
Everyone is waiting for you.

Moose

I never did see a moose.

I'm told at dawn or dusk
you might have luck
and glimpse one lurking
at the edge of the dark that hides
all things we long to see.

But even then, I tell you—
nothing but birdcall and fog
drift over this water.
Mobs of trees pray
the same prayer
we've known all along,
since we first looked
on the lucid morning,
expecting for no reason
a daily epiphany.

(What else are windows for?)

Still no moose on this lake.
I can't wait any longer.
I've places to be.

Maybe after I'm gone
one will brave the marshy bank,
plunge its furred muzzle
deep in the water
and come up dripping,
to stare my ghost
in the eye, as if to say,

You see? You see?
We do exist.

And my ghost replies,

Please don't hold a grudge—
even as I left this place
I never did give up
on glimpsing you
in the trees.

Chanterelles

After the night rain, shy chanterelles
in the shadow of pines.

We wandered into the woods with our baskets empty.
Stepped through crowds of wet berry bushes,
over moss that gave under our boots.

Like walking on water.

I wanted the word for moss.
Samanos, you said.

I wanted the word for fox. *Lapė*.

We saw our first chanterelle
bowing its tender, saffron head
beside a softening log.

Voveraitė, you said,
cutting its stalk with your knife.

All day we walked and gathered
mushrooms and words from the forest,

blueberry
  mėlynių
pine
  pušis
birch
  beržas,

until we grew hungry
and our baskets full.

That night we cooked our finds
in garlic, butter, and wine.
We ate them in the dark,

listening with our mouths
to the land's soft utterance.

In this way I learned, slowly,
to speak your tongue.

Vilnius to Warsaw, 2001

The train rattled on its long rails,
slow and erratic, not unlike history,
into banks of fog that obscured the view.
I shared my compartment with a giant,
I think of Estonian origin, with a friendly
brown mustache and fat but dainty hands
that tipped vials of vodka into cups for us,
as he talked and talked, in German
or Russian—I caught every tenth word—
about his bountiful business in automobiles.
He bought wrecked BMWs in the west,
then sold them to his countrymen. Any wrong
could be made right by his mechanic,
who was an angel of God. Did I believe
in God, he asked? And what of the euro?
Michael Jordan and the Chicago Bulls?
Ernest Hemingway, Old Man and Sea?
I did, I did believe, and understood that man
down to his jolly soul. We drank
to euros, to dollars, to Mercedes Benz.
Our train sped on, the dense fog lifted,
beds of nettles waved us westward.
The sun, as audacious as any lie ever told,
set fire to Poland's paper sky, while
my portly Estonian oracle revealed
the secrets of love in his mother tongue.
Warsaw soon swallowed us whole.
Oh, I didn't want us to leave
that boozy fantasy of camaraderie,
but he rose from his seat with a sigh
and in sensible English said good-bye.

Airspace in Wartime

Amid clouds claimed by no king,
my boy sketches the sky.

Below, Sweden slouches southward.
To the east, artillery barks at the wind.

In national archives, scholars amend
the long-told fiction of nations.

Flags snap to attention
as armies weep to their anthems.

Secretive stags dash across state lines.
Not even satellites see them.

Soon we will land in a country with a name,
borders, memorials, uncountable graves.

For now, we soar over unmapped waves
rumpling the surface of a patrolled sea.

Some vision spills from my son's pencil,
His sky fits on an airplane napkin—

a patch of cloud-fold and light,
a miniature flag of peace.

A Village No More

A village no more—
six houses on a hill, a dot
of ink on a fading map
in a distant attic.

It once had a name. Now
moss greens the shingles,
apples drop to the grass,
wasps drone to the rot.

The wind genuflects through
a broken pane into a parlor
where guests once talked
of children and weather.

A teacup waits on the mantle.
Inside its porcelain hollow,
a trace of tea and
crystallized honey.

On the wall, a calendar
charts the vanished future.
In the kitchen, the mother
of God hangs crooked on a nail.

Who held the hammer?
Whose eyes sought the Virgin's?
Whose wood burned to ash
in the cold furnace?

Outside, a deer leaps the gate.
She noses the fruit in the grass
and feeds on the clover.
How history sounds:

her teeth tearing
the thick, sweet tufts of growth.
The same weed prospers
on the far hill

among birch and stones
that bear the names
of the lucky ones, who died
in peace at home.

Lenin Square

In the center of the square,
in his cap of white,
Lenin awaits the dawn.

Snow dusts his bronze body, ice hangs
from a raised arm that points
and points toward a godless future.

An old man dares approach him.
He has come to feed the pigeons.
They flutter their wings in greeting.

In the dark conservatory,
a violinist looks out the window
at Lenin. He stares back

as she lifts her bow,
and breaks the silence
with her feverish scales.

Across the square, a lone soldier
guards the doors of a locked church.
He stomps his feet to stay warm.

If you listen closely,
you can hear him whisper
an impolitic Hail Mary.

You can hear crumbs
strewn on ice for the birds,
the violin's song,

and in the prison next door,
an executioner
sliding bullets into his pistol.

Arpeggios ascend,
crumbs scatter,
a soldier prays

as the prisoner falls
into his pooling blood,
and snow fills Lenin's eyes.

Such days—innumerable—have come
and gone, forgotten, as even
the deepest snows will melt.

The Remnant

He knows it is Christmas—
his radio told him so.

The city streets slick with ice,
and still he limps into the morning air.

His cane, a third leg, of sterner stuff than flesh.
His face, softened by nine decades of prayer.

How does a man older than church bells
measure time? Every Sunday

he makes this walk, Holy Days too,
each raised cobble a threat to his step.

He remembers both world wars
as if they were last night's dreams.

A soldier who shot bullets into clouds
so they would not find bodies.

His wife and sole companion
surveys his empty rooms

from the frame in which she hangs
on his cracked and cobwebbed wall.

He sees ahead the spires
of the church where he'll speak

to a God whose face comes
close enough, some nights, to kiss.

He has long wanted to die,
his pains older than most men.

His monstrous sins
long forgiven, long in flight

from what's left of his life—
it has curved into its final shape

a question mark kneeling
before the Son.

Criminals

We paddled out in our kayak
to the center of a lake made gold
by sunset. From the reeds
along the shadowed edge
came a disturbance—ripples,
the soft splash of fins
caught in a torn, tangled,
weed-strewn net

left forgotten by villagers
long ago—two fish,
their amber skins cut
on the string from thrashing
to get into the great water again.

We sliced open the net.

Bleeding from gills and tails,
barely alive, the fish
hung in black water,
yet swollen with life,
eyes and mouths
gaping.

We took them
into the belly of our boat.
On shore, we scraped off
the gold scales, scooped
out the guts, and made
a meal from those fish
caught by treachery,
found by chance.

They cooked up crisp
in the oil, delicious.

When it was all over,
we sat on shore,
stomachs full, and looked
into the dark water
like criminals.

Like a Thief in the Night

I once rode out of a Tatra valley
on a horse-pulled wagon
with a priest who joked of God
all the way to the Krakow train
on which I'd be robbed
of what little I owned
by an old woman who promised
to pray for my soul.

I do wish that priest had told me
a little something of the meaning
of just one of those peaks,
which I'd photographed with my soon-to-be
stolen camera, so sure of their importance.

Now I hear on the radio the Tatras
are no more.

They've changed their magnificent minds
about being mountains—got clear out
of the business—and were last seen
swimming in the Caspian Sea,

which itself has a famously precarious
grip on reality.

At least, the priest and I have stayed in touch.
He has written to say he's been defrocked
and spends his days mining fool's gold
from California rocks.

PS, he adds, *the Lord is coming
like a thief in the night.*

After All Souls Night

An uninvited guest that dawn,
I dared pass through the graveyard gate.

The women had all come and gone,
their candles burned to blackened nubs.

The pooled wax, once soft and hot,
had chilled and slickened with cold dew.

In grass beside one silent plot,
a crow picked out a trembling worm

and glanced at me and cawed and flew
to keep its watch atop a tree.

I strolled past graves weeded and strewn
with blooms, green wreaths, and wishful seeds.

The stones looked shy in dawn's grey glow,
as if unclothed by day's approach.

I stared at names of men below
the sod, whose wives and children had

lit wicks against their lasting doom,
pinpricks of flame to mark their faith,

to flare and smoke till morning's gloom
extinguished them with solemn light,

a light revealing what was there:
the graves, the crow, and waiting air.

The News from Norway

You come to my room with news of your death.
Your cousin has dreamed of you walking
into your grandmother's grave.

She greeted you with a kiss on your mouth
and held you and promised you
the troubles of life were no longer yours.

This dear cousin, dreaming in Norway.
Your grandmother's grave, at the edge of a Lithuanian wood.
And here are we on the ocean's far shore.

Do we share one death—his and hers and yours?
Are we one creature connected by a tissue of dreams,
by underground rivers fed with our tears?

Outside my room, where we sit discussing this news,
a noontime rain has paused and resumed its gentle soaking.
Soon it will pass and leave us in silence.

Neringa

When my soul hurts, I gather my bones
and carry them to the lake
where the fisherman lives.

He has trained the gray goslings to come when he calls.
They fly to his boat-side, and soar at his ear
as he plows through a field of deep water.

Their long necks shimmer
with tiny gray and white feathers,
their soft wings clap at the air.

The fisherman rests easy in the boat,
the map of the sun in his red face.

Follow his eyes to hills of grain.
There I will wander through rye,
scaring up blackbirds along a dusty road,

till I come to a city of towers.
On a high balcony, a woman hangs sheer stockings
stuffed with onions, gold and glossy.
She walks barelegged through her rooms humming.
Under her nails, the fertile black earth.

I rest a while on her bed.
I watch her arms as she brushes her hair.

On the table, a jar of pickles catches the sun.
We eat them. They taste of the sea,
of the March morning we swam in the surf—
rough glittering waves of tears.

We made love on a shore littered with shells
long since crushed into sand
and walked home arm in arm
over a carpet of moss.

We stopped among berries to feast
on their tart blue wisdom.
Don't you remember?
Our fingers turned purple.
Our kisses tasted of rain.

The Thread

I live in half a house,
half a man with half a wife.

We dream at night of half
a moon and half an earth.

Come morning we sew, we sew
our halves together with thread

spun from our half hearts.

The thread is tender, it is weak,
a gust of wind will tear it.

Over and over, the world
splits open beneath our feet.

We sew and sew each day
to keep our half-lives whole.

When we run out of thread—

oh, but then halves and wholes,
wholes and halves

will vanish in the
indivisible sky.

The Wrong House

Here somehow I have mistaken
a long dark block in a city that is not
at all my home for a street

elsewhere, in a town
far across the sea,
a littered stretch of road

where pigeons and hookers
in heels perhaps strut by still
and once at least there was a shop

where long ago I bought
an ounce or two of fresh
loose-leaf earl grey tea

to bring home to you.
The pot we made remains
fragrant in some chamber

of my mind, where the lamps
burn bright, the fire warms
our thighs, and we talk

of nothing. But what's this cold
street where the tea shop is not, is
never, and the doors are locked,

and you are not? Nor pigeons,
nor light to see but the glow
from an upstairs window.

It spills out dimly over me.
Behind the pane a pair
of young lovers kiss

perhaps over their own pot
of tea, its bouquet afloat
in their cozy room,

scenting their tender hour.
What did we say when
it was our turn, our hour?

What were our words?
Was that even me fixing the tea?
Was that even you?

My love, I cannot any longer
see our own faces, cannot hear
our voices. Are they up there

behind that lit glass?
Is that our life steeping
in the wrong house?

After the Funeral

To walk on sand, to walk on water,
my grandfather slowly limps
toward the surf the day his wife was burnt
to ash and stashed inside an urn.

Her name now escapes his grasp,
so too her face, and who is this woman
holding fast his hollow arm?
She claims to be his daughter.
Her mouth, so red, a mouth on fire.
Daughter? Father? Mother?
The gull's fierce screams make more sense
than do the words this woman sounds.

Sand pricks his soft cheeks, his speckled head.
A gust blows high his black funeral tie.
Sea oats bow down their necks to him
as the gull swoops low and defers
to his kingly lurch and roll
toward the waves that speak to him.

They speak so simply all the words
a man could need. An ever-percussive
prayer that prays in waves that crest
and blast all names to foam and smatter.
Black ocean chill flows through his lungs.
He takes it in and in, all the words
that ever were and all the love.

His wife: gone, yes, he knows.
Now he knows and loves and knows,
before again the darkness comes.

Clouds Like Muscles

Looking up the famous Auden poem
where the dogs go on with their doggy/life,
I notice on the inside cover
the words

      clouds like muscles

penned in faint blue ink
by my hand long ago.

I was in London then, new to Auden,
to Hampstead Heath and beer
and the weight of one-pound
coins in my pocket. *Clouds
like muscle*s perhaps I wrote
in Hyde Park or Vauxhall
or aboard a bus, while gawking
at a patch of ribboned sky.

I remember nothing of the sight,
or of that day, the tea
I might have sipped,
the streets I might have braved.
That hour, those rippling clouds,
that suffering boy with his paperback poems—

I wander back to him now
and sit beside him in the grass
along the Serpentine.

He knows nothing of all he will do.

I stay with him awhile
and let him confess his loneliness.
I remind him of what he will soon forget:
that even the ship in Auden's poem,
that saw Icarus fall to the sea,

Had somewhere to get to and sailed calmly on.

I tell him to remember his sorrow is small
and the sky above vast and strong.

Paul Jaskunas is the author of two works of fiction: *The Atlas of Remedies* (Stillhouse Press) and *Hidden* (Free Press). His writing has appeared in many periodicals, including the *New York Times, America, Tab, The Pierian,* and the *Potomac Review.* He is a past recipient of the Friends of American Writers Award, a Fulbright scholarship, and grants from the Maryland State Arts Council. Since 2008, Paul has taught literature and writing at the Maryland Institute College of Art, where he edits the art journal *Full Bleed.*

www.ingramcontent.com/pod-product-compliance
Lightning Source LLC
Chambersburg PA
CBHW020221090426
42734CB00008B/1156